The Amazing Keto Recipe Book for Women

Healthy and Tasty Keto Recipes to Boost Your Meals and Improve Your Lifestyle

Sebastian Booth

Table of contents

Cheesy Baked Jalapeño Peppers

Macros: Fat 73% | Protein 14% | Carbs 13%

Prep time: 30 minutes | Cook time: 30 minutes | Serves 15

B aked jalapeños taste better than fried ones. The recipe is rich in nutritional value and flavors from the eggs, cheese, milk, and mayonnaise. Enjoy this meal anytime you feel hungry.

1 cup Cheddar cheese

¼ cup keto-friendly mayonnaise

1 cup cream cheese

15 jalapeño peppers, halved lengthwise and seeded

½ tablespoon unsweetened almond milk

2 beaten eggs

1½ cups crushed almond

Cooking spray

1. Start by preheating the oven to 350ºF (180ºC) and spray a baking tray lightly with cooking spray. Set aside.
2. Mix the Cheddar cheese, mayonnaise, and cream cheese in a mixing bowl.
3. Fill the jalapeño halves with the cheese mixture.
4. In a small bowl, whisk together the milk and eggs, then put the crushed almonds in another bowl.

5. Dredge the stuffed jalapeño halves in the egg mixture completely, then roll in the crushed almonds for a good coating.
6. Arrange the coated jalapeños on the prepared baking tray.
7. Bake in the preheated oven until browned lightly, for about 30 minutes.
8. Remove from the oven and serve while still warm

STORAGE: Store in a wrapped plastic paper in the fridge for up to 4 days.

REHEAT: Microwave, covered, until the desired temperature is reached or reheat in an air fryer / instant pot, covered, on medium.

SERVE IT WITH: To make this a complete meal, serve the jalapeño peppers with blue cheese dressing.

PER SERVING

calories: 147 | fat: 12.1g | total carbs: 5.2g | fiber: 0.7g | protein: 5.4g

Keto Baked Eggs

Macros: Fat 60% | Protein 35% | Carbs 4%

Prep time: 5 minutes | Cook time: 10 minutes | Serves 1

The combination of ingredients in this meal makes it perfect whether it is breakfast, lunch, or dinner. Make this recipe with your preferred meat. It can be beef, pork, or lamb. If you have some leftover s, then you can use them.

3 ounces (85 g) cooked ground meat (beef, pork, or lamb)

2 eggs

2 ounces (57 g) shredded cheese

1. Start by preheating the oven to 400ºF (205ºC).
2. In a greased baking dish, put the cooked ground meat. Using a spoon to make two holes, then crack the eggs into the holes.
3. Top with a sprinkle of shredded cheese.
4. Bake in the oven for 15 minutes until the eggs are set.
5. Remove from the oven and cool for about 5 minutes before serving.

STORAGE: Store in an airtight container in the fridge for up to 4 days.

REHEAT: Microwave, covered, until the desired temperature is reached or reheat in a frying pan or air fryer, covered, on medium.

SERVE IT WITH: To make this a complete meal, serve the eggs with avocados and fresh herbs. The baked eggs also taste better with crunchy and crispy green salad.

PER SERVING

calories: 606 | fat: 40.8g | total carbs: 7.0g | fiber: 0g | protein: 41.0g

Mexican-Style Scrambled Eggs

Macros: Fat 68% | Protein 24% | Carbs 7%

Prep time: 5 minutes | Cook time: 10 minutes | Serves 4

P repare this dish for your breakfast. Filled with the flavorful eggs, tomatoes, jalapeños, and scallions, you will have wonderful breakfast moments to spice up your day.

1 ounce (28 g) butter

1 chopped tomato

1 chopped scallion

2 chopped pickled jalapeños pepper

6 eggs

Salt and freshly ground black pepper, to taste

3 ounces (85 g) shredded cheese

1. Put the butter in a medium pan over medium-high heat to melt.
2. Add the tomatoes, scallions, and jalapeños, then cook for 4 minutes until tender.
3. Beat the eggs in a small bowl, then add to the pan. Cook as you scramble for 2 minutes.
4. Sprinkle with the pepper, cheese, and salt. Stir well and serve warm.

STORAGE: Store in an airtight container in the fridge for up to 4 days.

REHEAT: Microwave, covered, until the desired temperature is reached or reheat in a frying pan, covered, on medium.

SERVE IT WITH: To make this a complete meal, serve the eggs with crisp lettuce, avocados, and a dressing to add taste.

PER SERVING

calories: 216 | fat: 16.7g | total carbs: 4.3g | fiber: 0.7g | protein: 12.2g

Fluffy Western Omelet

Macros: Fat 73% | Protein 23% | Carbs 4%

Prep time: 5 minutes | Cook time: 25 minutes | Serves 2

E njoy the fluffy filled with cheesy egg goodness omelet. This keto meal will fulfill our choices for dinner, lunch, or even breakfast. Filled with tasty flavors from bell pepper, ham, and onion, you will love it.

2 tablespoons heavy whipping cream or sour cream

6 eggs

Salt and freshly ground pepper, to taste

3 ounces (85 g) shredded cheese

2 ounces (57 g) butter

½ chopped green bell pepper

5 ounces (142 g) diced smoked deli ham

½ chopped yellow onion

1. Whisk the cream and eggs in a bowl until fluffy, then add the pepper and salt. Stir well.
2. Mix in half of the shredded cheese and set aside.
3. In a large pan, melt the butter over medium heat. Add the peppers, ham, and onions and fry for 5 minutes. Pour in the egg mixture and cook until it is almost firm, making sure not to burn the edges.

4. Reduce the heat to low, then top with the remaining cheese.
5. Transfer to a plate and slice in half before serving.

STORAGE: Store in an airtight container in the fridge for up to 4 days. It is not recommended to freeze.

REHEAT: Microwave, covered, until the desired temperature is reached or reheat in a frying pan, covered, on medium.

SERVE IT WITH: To make this a complete meal, serve the omelet with your preferred green salad. The omelet also goes well with jalapeños and low-carb Sriracha sauce.

PER SERVING

calories: 872 | fat: 71.3g | total carbs: 10.7g | fiber: 0.5g | protein: 46.9g

Homemade Cheddar Crackers

Macros: Fat: 67% | Protein: 29% | Carbs: 4%

Prep time: 15 minutes | Cook time: 20 minutes | Serves 4

One of the easy to make crackers that are totally addicting! These homemade crackers are super cheesy with a delicious kick.

1 cup almond flour

½ cup Cheddar cheese, shredded finely

1 tablespoon nutritional yeast

¼ teaspoon baking soda

¼ teaspoon garlic powder

¼ teaspoon sea salt

2 teaspoons olive oil

1 egg

Olive oil spray

1. Preheat your oven to 350°F (180°C) and line a baking sheet with parchment paper. Lightly grease two parchment papers with olive oil spray and set them aside.
2. In a large mixing bowl, add the almond flour, Cheddar cheese, nutritional yeast, baking soda, garlic powder, and salt and mix well. In a separate bowl, place the oil and egg, then beat until well combined.

Add the egg mixture into the bowl of flour mixture and with a wooden spoon, mix well until a dough ball forms.

3. On a flat work surface, knead the dough for 1 to 2 minutes with your hands. Arrange 1 greased parchment paper onto the work surface. Place the dough ball onto the greased parchment paper and with your hands, then press into a disk. Arrange another greased parchment paper on top of dough, then roll it into a 9×12-inch (⅛-inch thick) rectangle with a rolling pin. With a pizza cutter, cut the edges of the dough into an even rectangle. Now, cut the dough into 1½×1½-inch columns and rows. Arrange the crackers onto the prepared baking sheet. Bake for about 15 to 20 minutes or until crispy.
4. Remove from the oven to a wire rack to cool completely before serving.

STORAGE: Place the crackers in an airtight container and store at room temperature for up to 1 week.

SERVE IT WITH: Spread a thin layer of cream cheese over crackers and top with crispy bacon bits before serving.

PER SERVING

calories: 184 | fat: 13.8g | total carbs: 1.8g | fiber: 0.3g | protein: 7.2g

Cheesy Crab Stuffed Mushrooms

Macros: Fat: 75% | Protein: 21% | Carbs: 4%

Prep time: 15 minutes | Cook time: 17 minutes | Serves 6

A party favorite appetizer of stuffed mushrooms with a flavorsome filling... These mushrooms are stuffed with a flavorsome combination of crab meat, cream cheese, parmesan, almonds and herbs.

12 large button mushrooms, cleaned and stemmed

1 cup cooked crab meat, chopped

1 cup cream cheese, softened

½ cup Parmesan cheese, grated

¼ cup ground almonds

1 scallion, chopped

1 tablespoon fresh parsley, chopped

1 teaspoon garlic, minced

Olive oil spray

1. Preheat the oven to 375°F (190°C) and line a baking sheet with parchment paper.
2. Arrange the mushrooms onto the prepared baking sheet, stem-side up. Lightly spray them with olive oil spray. Bake in the preheated oven for about 2 minutes. Remove from the oven to a plate lined with paper towels to drain the grease.

3. Meanwhile, make the filling: In a large bowl, place the remaining ingredients and mix until well combined. Stuff each mushroom with about 1½ tablespoons of the filling mixture. Arrange the stuffed mushrooms onto the same baking sheet. Bake for about 14 to 15 minutes or until the mushrooms become bubbly and golden brown.
4. Remove the baking sheet from oven and serve warm.

STORAGE: You can store the filling in a container in the refrigerator for 1 to 2 days.

REHEAT: Microwave, covered, until the desired temperature is reached or reheat in a frying pan or air fryer / instant pot, covered, on medium.

SERVE IT WITH: Serve the stuffed mushrooms with the mashed broccoli or cauliflower.

PER SERVING

calories: 198 | fat: 15.9g | total carbs: 4.6g | fiber: 0.6g | protein: 10.2g

Sweet and Zesty Chicken Wings

Macros: Fat: 49% | Protein: 45% | Carbs: 6%

Prep time: 15 minutes | Cook time: 40 minutes | Serves 4

A lip-smacking recipe of sticky wings is ideal for a snack party! These chicken wings are baked in the oven until crispy and then coated with a sweet and zesty sauce.

WINGS:

2 pounds (907 g) chicken wings

2 tablespoons coconut oil, melted

SAUCES:

4 tablespoons butter

2 teaspoons garlic, minced

2 teaspoons fresh ginger, grated

2 to 3 tablespoons granulated monk fruit sweetener

3 to 4 tablespoons fresh lime juice

2 to 3 teaspoons lime zest, grated

1. Preheat the oven to 400°F (205°C) and line a baking sheet with parchment paper.
2. For the wings: In a large bowl, place the wings and coconut oil. Toss to coat well. Arrange the wings onto the prepared baking sheet in a single layer.

Bake for about 40 minutes, flipping once halfway through.

3. Meanwhile, make the sauce: In a small saucepan, melt the butter over medium-high heat and sauté the garlic and ginger for about 3 minutes. Stir in the monk fruit sweetener, lime juice and zest, then bring to a gentle boil. Reduce the heat to medium and cook for about 10 to 15 minutes or until it reaches the desired thickness, stirring frequently. Remove the saucepan from heat.
4. Remove the wings from the oven to a large bowl. Pour the sauce over the wings and serve warm.

STORAGE: In a resealable plastic bag, place the baked and then cooled chicken wings. Seal the bag and refrigerate for about 3 to 4 days.

REHEAT: Microwave, covered, until the desired temperature is reached or reheat in a frying pan or air fryer / instant pot, covered, on medium.

PER SERVING

calories: 474 | fat: 26.4g | total carbs: 6.9g | protein: 50.1g | fiber: 0.1g

Hearty Bacon and Mushroom Platter

Macros: Fat: 49% | Protein: 19% | Carbs: 33%

Prep time: 15minutes | Cook time: 15 minutes | Serves 4

A one-pan family favorite recipe of bacon and mushrooms... This easy to cook but richly delicious dish is prepared with only 5 ingredients.

6 uncured bacon strips, chopped

4 cups fresh wild mushrooms, sliced

2 teaspoons garlic, minced

2 tablespoons homemade chicken stock

1 tablespoon fresh thyme, chopped

1. Heat a large nonstick skillet over medium-high heat and cook the bacon for about 7 minutes or until crispy, stirring frequently. Add the mushrooms and garlic and sauté for about 7 minutes. Add the chicken stock and with the wooden spoon, stir to scrape up any browned bits from the bottom of skillet.
2. Remove from the heat and serve hot with fresh thyme sprinkled on top.

STORAGE: Store in an airtight container in the fridge for up to 4 days or in the freezer for up to 1 month.

REHEAT: Microwave, covered, until the desired temperature is reached or reheat in a frying pan or air fryer / instant pot, covered, on medium.

SERVE IT WITH: Serve this dish with your favorite greens.

TIP: Topping of Parmesan cheese will enhance the flavor of bacon and mushrooms.

PER SERVING

calories: 67 | fat: 3.9g | total carbs: 6.0g | fiber: 2.6g | protein: 3.9g

Keto Smoked Salmon Fat Bombs

Macros: Fat 90% | Protein 10% | Carbs 0%

Prep time: 10 minutes | Cook time: 0 minutes | Serves 12 Fat Bombs

S almon fat bombs are a combination of healthy fat like grass-fed butter, coconut oil, nut and the protein salmon. It provides an excellent keto diet with the low-carb content.

½ cup goat cheese, at room temperature

2 teaspoons freshly squeezed lemon juice

2 ounces (57 g) smoked salmon

Freshly ground black pepper, to taste

½ cup butter , at room temperature

1. Line a baking sheet with parchment paper and set aside.
2. Make the fat bombs: In a bowl, add cheese, lemon juice, smoked salmon, pepper, and butter, then stir well to blend.
3. Scoop 1 tablespoon of the butter mixture onto the baking sheet until you make 12 equally sized mounds.
4. Transfer the sheet into the refrigerator for about 3 hours until fat bombs become firm.

5. Remove from the refrigerator and let stand under room temperature for a few minutes before serving.

STORAGE: Store in an airtight container in the fridge for up to 4 days or in the freezer for up to 1 month.

SERVE IT WITH: To make this a complete meal, you can serve it with plain Greek yogurt.

PER SERVING

calories: 88 | fat: 9.0g | total carbs: 0g | fiber: 0g | protein: 1.9g

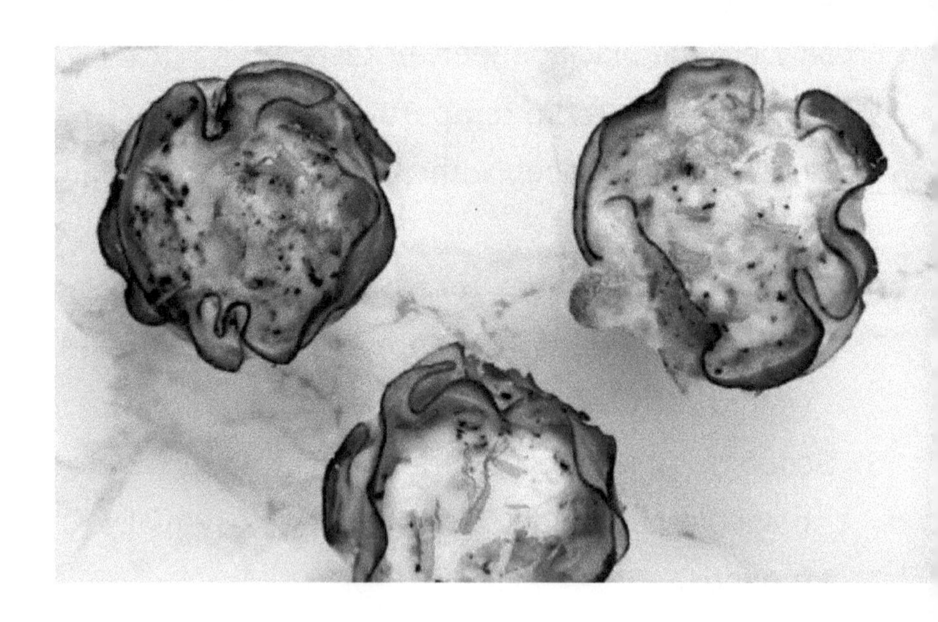

Deviled Eggs with Bacon and Cheese

Macros: Fat 80% | Protein 16% | Carbs 4%

Prep time: 15 minutes | Cook time: 0 minutes | Serves 12

The deviled eggs contain finely shredded Swiss cheese and bacon. They are nutritionally better than ordinary eggs. The recipe is easy and takes a short duration of time to cook.

6 large hard-boiled eggs, peeled

¼ cup keto-friendly mayonnaise

¼ cup finely shredded Swiss cheese

½ teaspoon Dijon mustard

¼ chopped avocado

Ground black pepper, to taste

6 cooked and chopped bacon slices

1. Cut the eggs in halves. Spoon the yolk out carefully and put in a bowl. Arrange the whites, hollow side facing up, on a plate.
2. Crumble the yolks with a fork. Add the mayonnaise, cheese, mustard, and avocado. Stir well to mix. Add the pepper to season.
3. Fill the hollow egg whites with the yolk mixture.
4. Top every egg half with the bacon before serving.

STORAGE: Store in an airtight container in the fridge for up to 4 days or in the freezer for up to 1 month.

REHEAT: Microwave, covered, until it reaches the desired temperature.

SERVE IT WITH: To make this a complete meal, serve with broccoli Cheddar soup.

PER SERVING

calories: 134 | fat: 11.9g | total carbs: 1.45g | fiber: 0.3g | protein: 5.2g

Crab–Stuffed Avocado

Macros: Fat 72% | Protein 17% | Carbs 11%

Prep time: 20 minutes | Cook time: 0 minutes | Serves 2

C rab-stuffed avocado salad is an amazingly delicious dish suitable for a light lunch. The meal is healthy, scrumptious, and filing. The stuffed crab goes well with the nutritive avocado.

1 halved lengthwise avocado, peeled and pitted

½ teaspoon freshly squeezed lemon juice

4½ ounces (127 g) Dungeness crab meat

¼ cup English cucumber, peeled and chopped

¼ cup red bell pepper, chopped

½ cup cream cheese

1 teaspoon cilantro, chopped

½ scallion, chopped

Sea salt and freshly ground black pepper, to taste

1. Brush the avocado edges with lemon juice, then set in a bowl.
2. In a bowl, add the crab meat, cucumber, red pepper, cream cheese, cilantro, scallion, salt, and pepper then stir to mix.
3. Divide the crab meat mixture in the avocado halves before serving.

STORAGE: Store in an airtight container in the fridge for up to 4 days or in the freezer for up to 1 month.

SERVE IT WITH: To make this a complete meal, serve the dish on a bed of greens.

PER SERVING

calories: 420 | fat: 32.0g | total carbs: 12.6g | fiber: 7.0g | protein: 16.8g

Cheddar Cheese Jalapeño Poppers

Macros: Fat 83% | Protein 13% | Carbs 4%

Prep time: 15 minutes | Cook time: 20 minutes | Serves 3

J alapeño poppers require few ingredients mainly bacon, jalapeño peppers and shredded Cheddar cheese. The yummy treat takes a short time to prepare.

5 slices bacon

6 jalapeño peppers

3 ounces (85 g) softened cream cheese

¼ teaspoon garlic powder

¼ cup Cheddar cheese, shredded

1. In a skillet over medium-high heat, add the bacon and fry for 3 to 4 minutes on each side until crispy. Allow the bacon to cool on a paper towel-lined plate.
2. Chop the bacon into ½-inch pieces.
3. Preheat the oven to 400°F (205°C) and line a rimmed baking sheet with parchment paper.
4. Slice the jalapeño peppers into halves. Using a spoon, scrap out the membranes and seeds.
5. In a bowl, use a fork to mix the cream cheese, garlic powder, Cheddar cheese, and bacon bits. Spoon the mixture into every jalapeño half, then arrange them on the lined baking sheet.

6. Bake in the preheated oven until the cheese melts for about 20 minutes and slightly crispy on top.
7. Transfer to serving plates to cool before serving.

STORAGE: Store in an airtight container in the fridge for up to 4 days or in the freezer for up to 1 month.

REHEAT: Microwave, covered, until it reaches the desired temperature.

SERVE IT WITH: To make this a complete meal, serve with a cup of zoodles or kelp pasta.

PER SERVING

calories: 314 | fat: 16.2g | total carbs: 3.5g | fiber: 0.8g | protein: 10.4g

Crispy Chicken

Macros: Fat 67% | Protein 32% | Carbs 2%

Prep time: 2 minutes | Cook time: 20 minutes | Serves 12

Chicken crisps are naturally crunchy dish that can be served for dinner. The meal is protein packed and takes a very short time to prepare. Everyone in the family will love it.

12 (9-ounces / 255-g) chicken thigh skins

SEASONING:

3 tablespoons coriander, ground

2 tablespoons gray sea salt, finely ground

1¼ teaspoons turmeric powder

¾ teaspoon celery seed, ground

¾ teaspoon parsley, dried

2 teaspoons mustard, ground

2 tablespoons onion powder

2 teaspoons paprika

½ teaspoon black pepper, ground

1. Preheat the oven to 325°F (160°C) and line a rimmed baking sheet with parchment paper.
2. Cut another parchment paper similar in size to the above and have a separate smaller baking sheet so

you can nestle the smaller baking sheet inside the bigger baking sheet.

3. Make the seasoning: In a ½-cup glass jar, add the coriander, salt, turmeric, celery, parsley, mustard, onion powder, paprika, and black pepper. Cover the jar, then shake.
4. In a bowl, transfer the chicken skins, then sprinkle 1 tablespoon of the seasoning. Toss until the skins are coated evenly.
5. On the larger baking sheet, arrange the skins evenly by placing them close.
6. Set the second parchment paper on the skins, then top with the smaller baking sheet to force the skins to remain in flattened state throughout the baking process.
7. Bake in the preheated oven until crispy for 20 minutes. Flip the chicken thigh skins halfway through.
8. Transfer the crisp chicken skins to serving plates to cool before serving.

STORAGE: Store in an airtight container in the fridge for up to 5 days or in the freezer for up to 1 month.

REHEAT: You can remove them from the freezer and enjoy immediately, or microwave, covered, until it reaches the desired temperature.

SERVE IT WITH: To make this a complete meal, serve with broccoli chowder soup.

PER SERVING

calories: 434 | fat: 32.2g | total carbs: 2.0g | fiber: 0.5g | protein: 32.2g

Easy Parmesan Chive and Garlic Crackers

Prep time: 40 minutes | Cook time: 15 minutes| Serves 4

Macros: Fat 72% | Protein 16% | Carbs 12%

P armesan chive and garlic crackers are perfect for holiday nights and weekday dinners. They are also perfect low-carb snacks for keto diet. The recipe is super easy and produces amazing results.

1 tablespoon olive oil

1 cup Parmesan cheese, finely grated

¼ cup chives, chopped

1 cup almond flour, blanched

½ teaspoon garlic powder

1 large egg, whisked

1 tablespoon butter, melted

SPECIAL EQUIPMENT:

A pastry cutter

1. Preheat the oven to 350ºF (180°C) and grease 2 large baking sheets with 1 tablespoon olive oil each.
2. In a bowl, add the cheese, chives, almond flour, and garlic powder and mix well to combine.
3. In another bowl, add the eggs and butter, then whisk them well.

4. Pour the egg mixture into the cheese mixture and blend well until you form a dough.
5. Divide dough into two equal portions and press well until they are ¼ inch thick.
6. Use a pastry cutter to slice each dough sheet into 25 equally sized crackers.
7. Lay the crackers onto the prepared baking sheets.
8. Bake in the preheated oven for 15 minutes until crispy. Turn off the oven and let the crackers rest for a few minutes before serving.

STORAGE: Store in an airtight container in the fridge for up to 4 days or in the freezer for up to 1 month.

REHEAT: Microwave, covered, until it reaches the desired temperature.

SERVE IT WITH: To make this a complete meal, serve with a cup of plain Greek yogurt.

PER SERVING

calories: 313 | fat: 26.4g | total carbs: 9.0g | fiber: 3.0g | protein: 12.9g

Low Carb Keto Sausage Balls

Macros: Fat 80% | Protein 17% | Carbs 4%

Prep time: 30 minutes | Cook time: 20 minutes | Serves 6

The keto sausage balls are the ideal low-carb snacks for various occasions. These sausage balls offer the best appetizers. The recipe has easy steps that make the snack simple to prepare.

2 tablespoons olive oil

1 cup almond flour, blanched

1 pound (454 g) bulk Italian sausage

1¼ cups shredded sharp Cheddar cheese

2 teaspoons baking powder

1 large beaten egg

1. Preheat the oven to 350ºF (180ºC) and grease a baking sheet with olive oil.
2. In a bowl, mix the flour, sausage, cheese, baking powder, and the egg.
3. Divide the mixture into 6 equal portions and roll to form into balls.
4. Transfer to the baking sheet and bake in the preheated oven until golden brown for about 20 minutes.
5. Transfer to a platter to cool before serving.

STORAGE: Store in an airtight container in the fridge for up to 4 days or in the freezer for up to 1 month.

REHEAT: Microwave, covered, until it reaches the desired temperature.

SERVE IT WITH: To make this a complete meal, serve with a cup of plain yogurt and a green salad.

PER SERVING

calories: 515 | fat: 46.2g | total carbs: 5.2g | fiber: 2.0g | protein: 21.2g

Mediterranean Baked Spinach with Cheese

Macros: Fat 75% | Protein 13% | Carbs 11%

Prep time: 5 minutes | Cook time: 25 minutes | Serves 6

S pinach gets a Mediterranean touch when baked in a casserole with a mixture of feta cheese with pitted black olives and butter. The recipe is easy to follow and takes a short time to prepare.

2 tablespoons olive oil

2 cups water

2 pounds (907 g) chopped spinach

4 tablespoons butter

Salt and black pepper, to taste

1½ cups grated feta cheese

½ cup halved and pitted black olives

4 teaspoons grated fresh lemon zest

1. Preheat the air fryer to 400ºF (205ºC) and grease the air fryer basket with olive oil.
2. In a pan, add water and bring to a boil. Add the spinach and blanch for about 4 minutes. Drain the excess water.
3. In a bowl, add the spinach, butter, salt, and black pepper and mix. Transfer to the air fryer basket and

cook for 15 minutes. Stir once halfway through the cooking time.

4. Transfer to serving bowls and add the cheese, olives, and lemon zest. Stir well before serving.

STORAGE: Store in an airtight container in the fridge for up to 3 days.

SERVE IT WITH: If you are a meat lover, you can enjoy this dish with roast chicken breasts or garlicky shrimp skewers; if you are a vegan, then you can serve it with a cup of green smoothie or a green salad.

PER SERVING

calories: 254 | fat: 21.9g | total carbs: 7.9g | fiber: 3.7g | protein: 9.8g

Cheesy Cauliflower Bake

Macros: Fat 82% | Protein 9% | Carbs 9%

Prep time: 5 minutes | Cook time: 30 minutes | Serves 6

T he cheesy cauliflower recipe takes a quick time to prepare. The cheesy cauliflower is a delicious way to make a low-carb and keto-friendly side dish that's packed with vegetables.

2 tablespoons olive oil

2 teaspoons avocado mayonnaise, keto-friendly

2 tablespoons mustard

2 chopped cauliflower heads

½ cup butter, chopped into ½-inch pieces

1 cup grated Parmesan cheese

1. Preheat the oven to 400ºF (205ºC) and grease a baking dish with olive oil.
2. In a bowl, add the avocado mayonnaise and mustard and mix well. Coat cauliflower heads with this mixture before placing in the baking dish.
3. Top with butter and Parmesan cheese and bake in the preheated oven until the cauliflower heads are soft for 25 minutes.
4. Transfer to serving plates to cool before serving.

STORAGE: Store in an airtight container in the fridge for up to 4 days or in the freezer for up to 1 month.

REHEAT: Microwave, covered, until it reaches the desired temperature.

SERVE IT WITH: To make this a complete meal, serve with Turmeric Beef Bone Broth.

PER SERVING

calories: 282 | fat: 26.2g | total carbs: 7.0g | fiber: 2.0g | protein: 6.8g

Easy Parmesan Roasted Bamboo Sprouts

Macros: Fat 67% | Protein 17% | Carbs 16%

Prep time: 8 minutes | Cook time: 15 minutes | Serves6

P armesan roasted bamboo sprouts are vegetarian-friendly and gluten-free. Pepper is added to the treat to spice it up. It takes a short time to prepare.

2 tablespoons olive oil

2 pounds (907 g) bamboo shoots

½ teaspoon paprika

Salt and black pepper, to taste

4 tablespoons butter

2 cups grated Parmesan cheese

1. Preheat the oven to 375ºF (190ºC) and grease a baking dish with olive oil.
2. Combine the bamboo shoots with paprika, salt, black pepper, and butter in a large bowl. Wrap the bowl in plastic and refrigerate to marinate for at least 1 hour.
3. Discard the marinade and transfer the bamboo sprouts to the baking dish and bake in the preheated oven for 15 minutes.
4. Transfer to serving plates to cool and top with cheese before serving.

STORAGE: Store in an airtight container in the fridge for up to 4 days or in the freezer for up to 1 month.

REHEAT: Microwave, covered, until it reaches the desired temperature.

SERVE IT WITH: To make this a complete meal, serve with chicken stuffed avocados.

PER SERVING

calories: 289 | fat: 21.9g | total carbs: 12.6g | fiber: 3.4g | protein: 13.5g

Cauliflower Bread Sticks with Cheese

Macros: Fat 76% | Protein 21% | Carbs 3%

Prep time: 10 minutes | Cook time: 20minutes | Serves 2

T he delicacy is gluten-free, low-carb and very simple to make. The treat has a very direct recipe that takes a short time to prepare. The crust can also be used for making pizza.

1 tablespoon olive oil

½ cup riced cauliflower

⅛ teaspoon ground oregano

⅛ teaspoon ground sage

⅛ teaspoon ground mustard

⅛ teaspoon thyme, dried

1 small beaten egg

½ cup freshly grated Monterey jack cheese

Salt and ground black pepper, to taste

Minced fresh parsley, for garnish

1. In a toaster oven, add the cauliflower and cook for 8 minutes or until soft.
2. In a bowl, add the cooked cauliflower. Add the oregano, sage, mustard, and thyme for seasoning.
3. Add the egg, ½ of cheese, salt and black pepper.

4. Preheat the oven to 450ºF (235°C) and grease a baking sheet with olive oil.
5. Arrange the cauliflower mixture on the greased baking sheet.
6. Bake in the preheated oven for 8 minutes. Top with remaining cheese and bake for an additional 5 minutes or until the cheese melts.
7. Remove from oven, garnish with parsley, and slice into sticks before serving

STORAGE: Store in an airtight container in the fridge for up to 4 days or in the freezer for up to 1 month.

REHEAT: Microwave, covered, until it reaches the desired temperature.

SERVE IT WITH: To make this a complete meal, serve with blackberry chocolate shake.

PER SERVING

calories: 218 | fat: 18.7g | total carbs: 1.8g | fiber: 0.6g | protein: 11.0g

Almond Fritters with Mayo Sauce

Macros: Fat 67% | Protein 18% | Carbs 15%

Prep time: 5 minutes | Cook time: 15 minutes | Serves 2

I know you do fancy fritters. You will realize that the ingredients reveal how nutritious the dish is. You will enjoy the flavors and the cheesy nature of the recipe. You will take less than 20 minutes to prepare the recipe.

FRITTERS:

1 ounce (28 g) fresh broccoli

1 small whisked egg

1 ounce (28 g) Mozzarella cheese

2 tablespoons plus 1 tablespoon flaxseed meal, divided

4 tablespoons almond flour

¼ teaspoon baking powder

Salt and freshly ground black pepper, to taste

SAUCE:

4 tablespoons fresh dill, chopped

4 tablespoons mayonnaise, keto-friendly

½ teaspoon lemon juice

Salt and freshly ground black pepper, to taste

1. Make the fritters: In a food processor, add the broccoli and process until chopped thoroughly.

2. In a bowl, add the processed broccoli, whisked egg, Mozzarella cheese, 2 tablespoons of flaxseed meal, almond flour, baking powder, black pepper and salt. Mix well to form batter. Divide and roll into 4 equal balls.
3. In a bowl, add the remaining 1 tablespoon of flaxseed meal. Dip the balls in this bowl to coat well.
4. Preheat an air fryer to 375ºF (190°C) and place balls in the basket.
5. Fry fritters until golden brown for 5 minutes. Transfer to a serving plate.
6. Make the sauce: In a bowl, add the dill, mayonnaise, lemon juice, salt, and pepper and mix well.
7. Dip the fritters into the sauce and serve.

STORAGE: Store in an airtight container in the fridge for up to 4 days or in the freezer for up to 1 month.

REHEAT: Microwave, covered, until it reaches the desired temperature.

SERVE IT WITH: To make this a complete meal, serve with keto tropical smoothie.

PER SERVING

calories: 381 | fat: 29.5g | total carbs: 17.7g | fiber: 9.6g | protein: 18.2g

Almond Sausage Balls

Macros: Fat 74% | Proteins 19% | Carbs 7%

Prep time: 30 minutes | Cook time: 25 minutes | Serves 6

W ith only five ingredients, get into the kitchen and prepare almond sausage balls within a few minutes. Take the keto balls anytime you feel hungry. Prepare in advance to save time. If you have kids, do not miss out on these tasty balls.

1 cup almond flour, blanched

3 ounces bulk Italian sausage

1¼ cups sharp Cheddar cheese, shredded

2 teaspoons baking powder

1 large egg

1. Start by preheating the oven to 350ºF (180ºC) then grease a baking tray.
2. In a mixing bowl, mix the almond flour, Italian sausage, Cheddar cheese, baking powder, and the egg until mixed evenly.
3. Make equal-sized balls out of the mixture, then put them on the baking tray.
4. Put in the oven and bake for 20 minutes or until golden brown.
5. Remove from the oven and serve.

STORAGE: Store in an airtight container in the fridge for up to 1 week.

REHEAT: Microwave, covered, until it reaches the desired temperature.

PER SERVING

calories: 266 | fat: 22.5g | total carbs: 4.7g | fiber: 2.0g | protein: 13.0g

Cheesy Keto Cupcakes

Macros: Fat 85% | Proteins 9% | Carbs 6%

Prep time: 10 minutes | Cook: 20 minutes | Serves 12

It requires few ingredients when preparing this recipe. Only six ingredients and you have your cupcakes ready. They are soft, tasty and delicious. Good, especially for kids.

¼ cup melted butter

½ cup almond meal

1 teaspoon vanilla extract

2 (8-ounce / 227-g) packages cream cheese, softened

¾ cup Swerve

2 beaten eggs

SPECIAL EQUIPMENT:

A 12-cup muffin pan

1. Start by preheating the oven at 350ºF (180ºC) then line a muffin pan with 12 paper liners.
2. In a mixing bowl, mix the butter and almond meal until smooth, then spoon the mixture into the bottom of the muffin cups. Press into a flat crust.
3. In a mixing bowl, combine vanilla extract, cream cheese, Swerve, and eggs.

4. Set the electric mixer to medium, then beat the mixture until smooth.
5. Spoon the mixture on top of the muffin cups.
6. Bake in the oven until the cream cheese is nearly set in the middle, for about 17 minutes.
7. Remove from the oven and let the cupcakes cool.
8. Once cooled, refrigerate for 8 hours to overnight before serving.

STORAGE: Store in an airtight container in the fridge for up to 1 days or in the freezer for up to 1 month.

REHEAT: Microwave, covered, until the desired temperature is reached or reheat in a frying pan or air fryer / instant pot, covered, on medium.

PER SERVING

calories: 169 | fat: 16.0g | total carbs: 2.7g | fiber: 0g | protein: 3.8g

Winter Cabbage and Celery Soup

Preparation Time: 5 minutes **Cooking Time:** 30 minutes **Servings**: 6

Ingredients:

- Tablespoon olive oil
- 2 cloves garlic, minced
- 1/2 head cabbage, shredded
- 2 stalks celery, chopped
- 1 grated tomato
- 3 cups bone broth preferable homemade
- 2 cups water
- **1/2 teaspoon ground black pepper**

Directions:

1. Heat the oil in a large pot over medium heat.
2. Sauté the garlic, celery and cabbage, stirring, for about 8 minutes.
3. Add grated tomato and continue to cook for further 2 - 3 minutes.
4. Pour the broth and water. Bring to a boil, lower heat to low, cover and simmer for 20 minutes or until cabbage softened.
5. Sprinkle with ground black pepper, stir and serve.

Nutrition:

- Calories 155 Total Fats 2g Carbs: 28g
- Protein 4g Dietary Fiber: 2.3g

Spinach Soup with Shiitake mushrooms

Preparation Time: 10 minutes

Cooking Time :15 minutes

Servings **: 6**

Ingredients **:**

- Tablespoon of olive oil
- 1 medium onion, chopped
- 2 cloves garlic, minced
- 2 cups of water
- 1/2 bunch of spinach
- 2 cups shiitake mushrooms, chopped
- 2 Tablespoon of almond flour
- 1 Tablespoon of coconut aminos
- 1 teaspoon coriander dry
- 1/2 teaspoon of ground mustard
- Salt and ground black pepper to taste

Directions **:**

1. Heat the olive oil and sauté the garlic and onion until golden brown.
2. Add the coconut aminos and the mushrooms and stir for a few minutes.
3. Pour water, chopped spinach and all remaining ingredients.

4. Cover and cook for 5 - 6 minutes or until spinach is tender.
5. Taste and adjust salt and the pepper.
6. Stir for further 5 minutes and remove for the heat.
7. Serve hot.

Nutrition:

- Calories 214 Total Fats 2g Carbs: 24g
- Protein 10g Dietary Fiber: 2.3g

Vegan Artichoke Soup

Preparation Time : 15 minutes

Cooking Time: 1 hour 5 minutes

Servings **: 6**

Ingredients **:**

- 1 Tablespoon of butter
- 2 artichoke hearts, halved
- 2 cloves garlic, minced
- 1 small onion, chopped
- 1 cup bone broth
- 2 cups of water
- 2 Tablespoon of almond flour
- Salt and ground black pepper to taste
- 2 Tablespoon of olive oil
- Fresh chopped parsley to taste
- **Fresh chopped fresh basil to taste**

Directions **:**

1. Heat the butter in a large pot, and add artichoke hearts, garlic and chopped onion.
2. Stir and cook until artichoke hearts tender.
3. Add bone broth, water and almond flout: season with the salt and pepper.
4. Bring soup to boil and cook for 2 minutes.

5. Add little olive oil, parsley and basil, stir and cook uncovered for 1 hour.
6. When ready, push the soup through sieve.
7. Taste and adjust salt and pepper.
8. Serve.

Nutrition:

- Calories: 252
- Carbohydrates: 21.9g
- Protein: 4.5g
- Fat: 17.7g
- Sugar: 0g
- Sodium: 58mg

Seafood Soup

Preparation Time: 10 minutes

Cooking Time :25 minutes

Servings : 6

Ingredients :

- 1/2 cup of olive oil
- 1 spring onion cut in cubes
- Tablespoon of fresh celery, chopped
- 2 cloves of garlic minced
- 1 tomato, peeled and grated
- 2 bay leaves
- 1 teaspoon of anise
- 6 Large, raw shrimps
- 1 sea bass and 1 sea bream fillets cut in pieces; about 1 1/2 lbs.
- 1 lb. mussels, rinsed in plenty of cold water
- Salt and ground black pepper
- Tablespoon of chopped parsley for serving
- **6 cups of water**

Directions :

1. Heat the olive oil in a large pot and sauté in the onion, garlic and celery for 4 -5 minutes over medium heat.

2. Add bay leaves, anise and grated tomato; stir and cook for further 5 minutes.
3. Add seafood and fish and pour 6 cups of water; season with little salt and pepper.
4. **Cover and cook for 10 - 12 minutes on low heat. Serve hot with chopped parsley.**

Nutrition:

- Calories: 546 Carbohydrates: 21.9g
- Protein: 18.6g Fat: 43.1g Sugar: 0.8g Sodium: 678mg

Hot Spicy Chicken

Preparation time **: 5 minutes** Cooking time **: 25 minutes**

Servings: **6**

Ingredients

- ¼ tbsp fennel seeds, ground
- ¼ tsp smoked paprika
- ½ tsp hot paprika
- ½ tsp minced garlic
- **2 chicken thighs, boneless**

Directions

1. Turn on the oven, then set it to 325 degrees F and let it preheat.
2. Prepare the spice mix and for this, bring out a small bowl, add all the ingredients in it, except for chicken, and stir until well mixed.
3. **Brush the mixture on all sides of the chicken, rub it well into the meat, then place chicken onto a baking sheet and roast for 15 to 25 minutes until thoroughly cooked, basting every 10 minutes with the drippings.**

Nutrition : Calories: 205 - Carbohydrates: 36.2g - Protein: 4.3g - Fat: 5.3g - Sugar: 2.8g - Sodium: 463mg

Bacon-Wrapped Jalapeno Poppers

Macros: Fat 81% | Protein 15% | Carbs 5%

Prep time: 30 minutes | Cook time: 30 minutes | Serves 30

I f you are looking for a snack that is packed with a bit of punch, look no further. These mouth-watering party favorite bites will please your taste buds and everyone in your family or party will love them.

2 (12-ounce / 340-g) packages ground sausage

2 (8-ounce / 227-g) packages cream cheese, softened

30 jalapeño chile peppers

1 pound (454 g) sliced bacon, halved

SPECIAL EQUIPMENT:

Toothpicks, soaked for at least 30 minutes

1. Preheat your oven to 375°F (190°C). Line a baking sheet with parchment paper and set aside.
2. Meanwhile, cook the sausages in a large skillet over medium-high heat until it's evenly browned, for about 12 minutes.
3. Drain the cooked sausages and transfer them to a mixing bowl. Add the cream cheese and stir until well combined. Set aside.
4. On a flat work surface, slice the jalapeños lengthwise and remove the seeds. Using a spoon to stuff the

jalapeño halves with uniform sausage and cream cheese filling. Wrap each stuffed jalapeño half with a half slice of bacon, then secure with a toothpick.

5. Arrange the stuffed jalapeños on the baking sheet and bake in the oven for 20 minutes, or until the bacon is crispy.
6. Remove from the oven and cool for about 5 minutes before serving.

STORAGE: Store in an airtight container in the fridge for up to 4 days or in the freezer for up to 1 month.

REHEAT: Microwave, covered, until it reaches the desired temperature.

SERVE IT WITH: To make this a complete meal, serve it with ranch dressing for dipping.

PER SERVING

calories: 197 | fat: 18.4g | total carbs: 1.8g | fiber: 0.4g | protein: 6.2g

Keto Bacon-Wrapped Barbecue Shrimp

Macros: Fat 79% | Protein 18% | Carbs 3%

Prep time: 20 minutes | Cook time: 10 minutes | Serves 4

T his keto bacon-wrapped barbecue shrimp is a hit when served as an appetizer or for dinner. Use large shrimps for a most satisfaction. Kick up its flavors by serving it with spicy sriracha mayo dip.

16 large shrimps, peeled and deveined

8 bacon slices, halved lengthwise

Barbecue seasoning to taste, keto-friendly

SPECIAL EQUIPMENT:

Toothpicks, soaked for at least 30 minutes

1. Preheat your oven to 450°F (235°C).
2. On a clean work surface, tightly wrap each shrimp with half slice of bacon, then secure with a toothpick.
3. Line your jelly roll pan with foil and position a baking rack in it.
4. Arrange the bacon-wrapped shrimp on a wire rack and generously sprinkle the barbecue seasoning on both sides. The rack prevents the shrimp from sitting on draining bacon fat when baking.
5. Allow to rest for 15 minutes, or until the bacon turns a little opaque after soaking in the seasoning.

6. Bake in the oven for 10 to 15 minutes, or until the shrimp is opaque and bacon is crispy.
7. Remove from the oven and cool for 5 minutes before serving.

STORAGE: Store in an airtight container in the fridge for up to 4 days. It is not recommended to freeze.

REHEAT: Microwave, covered, until it reaches the desired temperature.

SERVE IT WITH: To make this a complete meal, serve it with some keto veggies.

PER SERVING

calories: 238 | fat: 20.7g | total carbs: 1.1g | fiber: 0.1g | protein: 10.4g

Keto Cheddar Cheese and Bacon Stuffed Mushrooms

Macros: Fat 79% | Protein 17% | Carbs 4%

Prep time: 15 minutes | Cook time: 30 minutes | Serves 8

M ake your next family gathering hosting opportunity a breeze with this cheese and bacon stuffed mushrooms. They are deceptively simple, fast to prepare and tastier than you can imagine.

3 bacon slices

8 cremini mushrooms

1 tablespoon butter

1 tablespoon onions, chopped

¾ cup shredded Cheddar cheese, divided

1. Cook the bacon in a large skillet over medium-high heat until evenly browned, for about 12 minutes.
2. Transfer to a plate lined with paper towels to drain the excess grease. When cool enough to handle, crumble and set it aside.
3. Preheat your oven to 400°F(205°C).
4. Remove the mushrooms stems and chop them on your cutting board. Reserve the caps on a platter and set aside.

5. Melt the butter in the skillet over medium-high heat. Add the chopped mushroom stems and onions, then cook until the onions are tender.
6. Remove from the heat to a mixing bowl.
7. Put the crumbled bacon and ½ cup of Cheddar cheese in the mixing bowl. Stir to combine well.
8. Use a spoon to scoop the bacon filling to the mushroom caps.
9. Bake the stuffed caps in the oven for 15 minutes, or until the cheese melts.
10. Remove from the oven and sprinkle the remaining cheese on top for garnish and serve.

STORAGE: Store in an airtight container in the fridge for up to 4 days or in the freezer for up to 1 month.

REHEAT: Microwave, covered, until the desired temperature is reached or reheat in a frying pan or instant pot, covered, on medium.

SERVE IT WITH: To make this a complete meal, serve it with a cup of coffee.

PER SERVING

calories: 107 | fat: 8.9g | total carbs: 0.95g | fiber: 0.2g | protein: 4.3g

Easily Baked Buffalo Chicken Dip

Macros: Fat 80% | Protein 17% | Carbs 3%

Prep time: 15 minutes | Cook time: 20 minutes | Serves 8

I f you are tired of showing up at every super bowl party with a large bag of chips, then this is buffalo chicken dip will get you from snack shrub to an all-star appetizer. It's immensely delicious and very easy to put together.

3 cups rotisserie chicken , diced and cooked

2 (8-ounce / 227-g) packages cream cheese, softened

½ cup blue cheese dressing

¾ cup hot pepper sauce

½ tablespoon seafood seasoning

½ cup plus 2 tablespoons shredded pepper Jack cheese

½ cup crumbled blue cheese

Cayenne pepper, to taste

1. Preheat your oven to 400°F (205°C).
2. In a large bowl, mix the chicken, cream cheese, blue cheese dressing, hot pepper sauce, seafood seasoning, ½ cup of pepper Jack cheese, crumbled blue cheese, and cayenne pepper.
3. Transfer the mixture to a greased baking dish and top with 2 tablespoons pepper Jack cheese.

4. Bake for 15 to 20 minutes or until the dip is lightly browned.
5. Remove from the oven and garnish with cayenne pepper to serve.

STORAGE: Store in an airtight container in the fridge for 3 days.

REHEAT: Microwave, covered, until it reaches the desired temperature.

SERVE IT WITH: To make this a complete meal, serve it with some zucchini crisps.

PER SERVING

calories: 450 | fat: 37.2g | total carbs: 5.3g | fiber:0.2g | protein: 23.3g

Tasty Artichoke Dip

Macros: Fat 86% | Protein 9% | Carbs 5%

Prep time: 10 minutes | Cook time: 25 minutes | Serves 30

T his is one of the easiest and delicious chafing-dish dips you can make in your home. It's the best baked dip and a huge hit to serve your family and friends.

1 (6½-ounce / 184-g) jar marinated artichoke hearts, drained and quartered

1½ cups grated Parmesan cheese, divided

1 cup keto-friendly mayonnaise

1 (4-ounce / 113-g) can chopped green chile pepper

1 (8-ounce / 227-g) package cream cheese, softened

1. Preheat your oven to 350°F (180°C).
2. Combine the artichoke hearts, 1 cup Parmesan cheese, mayonnaise, chile pepper, and cream cheese in a mixing bowl. Stir to incorporate.
3. Spoon the artichoke mixture into a greased baking pan, and sprinkle with the remaining Parmesan cheese.
4. Bake in the oven for 25 minutes, or until the top is lightly browned.
5. Remove from the oven and serve warm.

STORAGE: Store in an airtight container in the fridge up to 4 to 5 days.

REHEAT: Microwave, covered, until it reaches the desired temperature.

SERVE IT WITH: To make this a complete meal, serve it with cucumber pieces or celery sticks.

PER SERVING

Calories: 73 | Fat: 6.3g | Total Carbs: 2.0g | Fiber: 0.4g | Protein: 2.2g

Spinach and Cheese Stuffed Mushrooms

Macros: Fat 85% | Protein 9% | Carbs 6%

Prep time: 15 minutes | Cook time: 55 minutes | Serves 12

S pinach and cheese stuffed mushrooms are flavor packed keto appetizer. The mushrooms are stuffed with cheese, spinach and vibrant garlic to make a recipe that for sure will impress.

5 tablespoons melted butter, divided

5 bacon slices

1 (10-ounce / 284-g) package frozen spinach, chopped

¼ cup water

12 large mushrooms

2 garlic cloves, minced

2 tablespoons chopped onion

4 cups heavy cream

½ cup grated Parmesan cheese

Salt and freshly ground pepper, to taste

1. Preheat your oven to 400°F (205°C). Grease a baking dish with 2 tablespoons of melted butter and set aside.
2. In a large skillet, cook the bacon over medium-high heat for 12 minutes until evenly browned, flipping occasionally.

3. Transfer to a plate lined with paper towels to absorb the excess grease. When cool enough to handle, crumble it and set aside.
4. Add the spinach in a saucepan, then add ¼ cup of water. Bring the water to a boil, then cook the spinach over medium heat for about 10 minutes.
5. Remove the spinach from the heat and drain the water. Set aside.
6. On a flat work surface, remove stems from the mushrooms and chop them. Reserve the chopped stems in a bowl, then arrange the caps on the prepared baking dish.
7. Heat the remaining butter in the saucepan over medium heat. Add the garlic and onions, then cook for 3 to 5 minutes, or until the onions are tender.
8. Stir in the cooked bacon, spinach, mushroom stems, and heavy cream, then bring them to a boil. Remove from the heat to another bowl.
9. Add the cheese, salt, and pepper. Stir with a fork until well combined. Using a spoon, scoop the mixture into the mushroom caps.
10. Bake in the oven for 30 minutes or until the cheese melts.
11. Remove from the oven and serve on a plate.

STORAGE: Store in an airtight container in the fridge up to 3 days. It is not recommended to freeze.

REHEAT: Microwave, covered, until the desired temperature is reached or reheat in an air fryer, covered, on medium.

SERVE IT WITH: The leftovers can be served with baked chicken as a side dish.

PER SERVING

calories: 239 | fat: 23.6g | Total carbs: 3.63g | fiber: 0.8g | protein: 4.76g

Balsamic Mushrooms

Macros: Fat 73% | Protein 8% | Carbs 19%

Prep time: 15 minutes | Cook time: 10 minutes | Serves 8

B alsamic mushrooms are yummy and a brilliant way to kick off your dinner party. The mushrooms are equally mouthwatering whether you serve them warm or cold. This means you can prepare them ahead of appetizer time.

3 tablespoons olive oil

3 minced garlic cloves

1 pound (454 g) mushrooms, freshly sliced

3 tablespoons balsamic vinegar

Salt and pepper, to taste

1. Heat the olive oil in a skillet and sauté the garlic for about 2 minutes. Make sure you do not brown the garlic.
2. Fold in the mushrooms and continue to cook as you stir for 3 minutes. Add the vinegar and cook for 2 minutes more. Lightly season with salt and pepper.
3. Remove from the heat and serve on a plate.

STORAGE: Store in an airtight container in the fridge up to 3 to 5 days.

REHEAT: Microwave, covered, until it reaches the desired temperature.

SERVE IT WITH: To make this a complete meal, serve it with a grilled steak or pork chops.

PER SERVING

calories: 64 | fat: 5.3g | total carbs: 3.25g | fiber: 0.6g | protein: 1.89g

Baba Ghanoush

Macros: Fat 66% | Protein 9% | Carbs 25%

Prep time: 5 minutes | Cook time: 40 minutes | Serves 12

This Baba Ghanoush is a creamy and flavorful dip that you can make at your home with very few preparations. It highly complements keto diet and can even be served as vegan, Whole30, and gluten-free diets.

1 eggplant

¼ cup tahini

¼ cup lemon juice

2 garlic cloves, minced

2 tablespoons sesame seeds

Salt and pepper, to taste

1 ½ tablespoon olive oil

Cooking spray

1. Preheat your oven to 400°F (205°C) and lightly grease the baking sheet with cooking spray.
2. Arrange the eggplant on the greased baking sheet and use a fork to poke holes in the skin.
3. Roast the eggplant for 40 minutes until tender, turning it over occasionally.
4. Remove from the oven to a bowl with cold water. Drain the water and peel off the skin.

5. Process the eggplant, tahini, lemon juice, garlic, and sesame seeds in a food processor until smooth. Sprinkle the salt and pepper to season.
6. Place the mixture in a serving bowl, then add the olive oil. Mix well.
7. Chill in the refrigerator for about 3 hours before serving.

STORAGE: Store in an airtight container in the fridge up to 4 days.

SERVE IT WITH: To make this a complete meal, serve it with spinach or kale crisps.

PER SERVING

calories: 72 | fat: 5.3g | total carbs: 4.5g | fiber: 2.0g | protein: 1.6g

Cheesy Cauliflower Crackers

Macros: Fat 63% | Protein 28% | Carbs 9%

Prep time: 20 minutes | Cook time: 25 minutes | Serves 18

I t is a keto cracker that is spicy. It is perfect since it is a low-carb meal. It's delicious and a must-try recipe. It is also cheesy and sweet as it is enriched with the salad dressing and pepper.

1 (12-ounce / 340-g) package frozen riced cauliflower

1/2 teaspoon cayenne pepper

1 tablespoon dry ranch salad dressing mix

1 egg, whisked

1 cup shredded Parmesan cheese

1. Preheat the oven to 425ºF (220ºC). Line a baking sheet with parchment paper and set aside.
2. In a microwave-safe bowl, put the riced cauliflower. Microwave it for about 4 minutes. Set aside to cool for 15 minutes.
3. In a separate bowl, mix the riced cauliflower, cayenne pepper, ranch mix, and whisked egg. Stir well. Add the Parmesan cheese, then mix well until it is incorporated.
4. Make the crackers: Scoop about 2 tablespoons of the mixture onto the prepared baking sheet one at a

time and flatten each to about ⅛ -inch thickness with a rolling pin.

5. Transfer to the oven and bake for about 10 minutes. Flip the crackers over and bake for 10 minutes more, then place them on a wire rack to cool. Serve warm.

STORAGE: Store in an airtight container in the fridge for up to 4 days or in the freezer for up to 1 month.

REHEAT: Microwave, covered, until it reaches the desired temperature.

SERVE IT WITH: To make this a complete meal, serve the dish with Keto Broccoli Cheddar Soup.

PER SERVING

calories: 80 | fat: 3.0g | total carbs: 9.8g | fiber: 4.4g | protein: 5.9g

Deviled Mayonnaise Eggs

Macros: Fat 69% | Protein 25% | Carbs 6%

Prep time: 10 minutes | Cook time: 20 minutes | Serves 8

T he meal is perfect for gatherings such as holidays and the Easter. The ingredients are simple and easy to prepare. The paprika pops the flavor of the meal. It is a healthy appetizer or a snack.

8 eggs

⅓ cup keto-friendly mayonnaise

2 tablespoons horseradish sauce

2 tablespoons low-carb Worcestershire sauce

1 teaspoon hot pepper sauce

Salt and pepper to taste

1 teaspoon paprika, for garnish

1 teaspoon dried parsley flakes, for garnish

1. Put the eggs in a saucepan of water and allow to boil for 7 minutes. Remove the eggs from the hot water with a slotted spoon. Let them cool under running cold water in the sink. Peel the eggs and place them on a plate.
2. Halve the eggs and put the yolks in a bowl. Reserve the egg whites on the plate. Using a fork, mash the egg yolks until finely smooth.

3. Add the mayonnaise, horseradish sauce, Worcestershire sauce, hot sauce, pepper, and salt. Stir to combine well.
4. Using a plastic bag, spoon in the yolk mixture. Snip off one corner to make a ½-inch opening and pipe the yolk filling into each halved egg white. Garnish with paprika and parsley before serving.

STORAGE: Store in an airtight container in the fridge for up to 4 days.

REHEAT: Microwave, covered, until it reaches the desired temperature.

SERVE IT WITH: To make this a complete meal, serve the dish with keto chicken soup.

PER SERVING

calories: 164 | fat: 12.9g | total carbs: 2.2g | fiber: 0.2g | protein: 9.2g

Tomatoes and Jalapeño Salsa

Macros: Fat 8% | Protein 11% | Carbs 81%

Prep time: 10 minutes | Cook time: 0 minutes | Serves 4

I t is an easy to make a recipe that takes only 10 minutes to prepare. The ingredients you use are fresh with lots of nutrients. Best when served immediately after preparation.

4 chopped large tomatoes

½ cup chopped fresh cilantro

1 chopped onion

3 cloves minced garlic

1 diced tomatillo

Salt, to taste

1 tablespoon lime juice

1 minced jalapeño pepper

1. Using a bowl, mix the tomatoes, cilantro, onion, garlic, tomatillo, salt, lime juice and jalapeño pepper. Stir to incorporate.
2. Cover the salsa with plastic wrap. Allow to chill until ready to serve or up to 24 hours.

STORAGE: Store in an airtight container in the fridge for up to 4 days. It is not recommended to freeze.

SERVE IT WITH: To make this a complete meal, serve the dish with zucchini chips.

PER SERVING

calories: 56 | fat: 0.5g | total carbs: 12.3g | fiber: 3.1g | protein: 2.4g

Buttered Lobster and Cream Cheese Dip

Macros: Fat 83% | Protein 15% | Carbs 2%

Prep time: 10 minutes | Cook time: 0 minutes | Serves 16

A delicious meal that is suitable when you prepare it a day before eating it. It is creamy and sweet to the taste buds. Why not try this simple recipe?

1 (7-ounce / 198-g) can drained and flaked lobster meat

1 tablespoon lemon juice

1 tablespoon minced onion

4 tablespoons softened butter

1 (8-ounce / 227-g) package softened cream cheese

Salt and freshly ground black pepper, to taste

1. In a bowl, add the lobster meat, lemon juice, onion, butter, cream cheese, pepper, and salt. Mix well until the mixture is smooth.
2. Cover the mixture with plastic wrap, then transfer to the refrigerator and chill until ready to serve.

STORAGE: Store in an airtight container in the fridge for up to 4 days.

SERVE IT WITH: To make this a complete meal, serve it with Bacon Cauliflower Chowder.

PER SERVING

calories: 85 | fat: 7.8g | total carbs: 0.7g | fiber: 0g | protein: 3.0g

Prosciutto and Asparagus Wraps

Macros: Fat 21% | Protein 51% | Carbs 28%

Prep time: 15 minutes | Cook time: 15 minutes | Serves 4

I t is a special and easy to make a meal. It is suitable for Mother's Day, Easter or any special occasion. When served, the meal is fancy and appealing to the eyes. The salty flavor complements the sweet asparagus flavor.

½ pound (227 g) sliced prosciutto

½ (8-ounce / 227-g) package softened Parmesan cheese

12 spears trimmed fresh asparagus

1. Preheat the oven to 450ºF (235ºC).
2. On a flat work surface, spread the prosciutto slices with the cheese. Tightly wrap the slices around 3 asparagus spears. Repeat with the remaining slices and asparagus spears.
3. Arrange the wrapped spears on a greased baking sheet in a single layer.
4. Transfer to the oven and bake for about 15 minutes until the asparagus spears become tender.
5. Transfer to four serving plates and cool for a few minutes before serving.

STORAGE: Store in an airtight container in the fridge for up to 4 days.

REHEAT: Microwave the sliced prosciutto, covered, until it reaches the desired temperature.

SERVE IT WITH: To make this a complete meal, serve the dish with Creamy Broccoli Cheddar Soup.

PER SERVING

calories: 178 | fat: 4.3g | total carbs: 12.6g | fiber: 0.2g | protein: 22.1g

Low-Carb Cheesy Almond Biscuits

Macros: Fat 72% | Protein 25% | Carbs 3%

Prep time: 20 minutes | Cook time: 20 minutes | Serves 8

T he biscuits are delicious. For cheese lovers, you won't miss out your favorite cheese. It can make individual biscuits or a large loaf. The biscuits are perfect for both keto and non-keto diet individuals.

1 tablespoon baking powder

2 cups almond flour

2½ cups shredded Cheddar cheese

4 eggs

⅛ cup heavy cream

1. Preheat the oven to 350ºF (180ºC) and line a baking sheet with parchment paper. Set aside.
2. In a bowl, add the baking powder, almond flour and Cheddar cheese. Stir well to mix. In a separate bowl, whisk the eggs until frothy.
3. Make a well in the center of the almond mixture bowl, then gently pour in the whisked eggs and heavy cream. Using a fork, stir the mixture until it forms a sticky batter.
4. Make the biscuits: Divide the batter into 9 equal portions and transfer to the baking sheet, then form

into a rounded biscuit shape. Bake for 20 minutes until a toothpick inserted in the center comes out clean.

5. Divide the biscuits among serving plates and allow to cool for 5 minutes before serving.

STORAGE: Store in an airtight container in the fridge for up to 4 days.

REHEAT: Microwave, covered, until it reaches the desired temperature.

SERVE IT WITH: To make this a complete meal, serve the biscuits with a cup of coffee.

PER SERVING

calories: 243 | fat: 19.7g | total carbs: 2.1g | fiber: 0.1g | protein: 14.5g

Buttered Coconut Puffs

Macros: Fat 87% | Protein 10% | Carbs 3%

Prep time: 0 minutes | Cook time: 40 minutes | Serves 2

I t has simple ingredients that can be prepared in no time. They are basic and sweet. The meal is versatile as it can complement a number of different foods. It can be taken as breakfast or dinner.

1 tablespoon olive oil, for greasing the cookie sheet

¼ cup butter

½ cup water

½ cup coconut flour

2 eggs

A handful of spiced fennel, for filling

1. Preheat the oven to 375ºF (190ºC) and grease the cookie sheet with olive oil. Set aside.
2. Heat the butter and water in a saucepan over medium heat until the butter melts. Pour the flour into the saucepan all at once. Vigorously stir until it forms a ball in the middle of the pan. Set aside.
3. Add the eggs, one at a time, then beat the mixture until fully blended and stiff. Drop about ¾ teaspoon portions onto the cookie sheet. Gently smooth the

pointed peaks with a moistened finger, and round the tops to ensure even rising.

4. Bake for about 40 minutes until puffs rise and are golden brown on top. Transfer to a wire rack to cool completely.
5. Slit an opening on one side, then stuff with the filling before serving.

STORAGE: Store in an airtight container in the fridge for up to 3 days.

SERVE IT WITH: To add more flavors to this meal, you can serve sprinkled with coconut flakes.

PER SERVING

calories: 404 | fat: 39.5g | total carbs: 3.3g | fiber: 0.7g | protein: 9.6g

Baked Beef, Pork and Veal Meatballs

Macros: Fat 74% | Protein 24% | Carbs 2%

Prep time: 30 minutes | Cook time: 30 minutes | Serves 8

T he combination of the beef, veal, and pork sound perfect, right? The mixture makes the meal very delicious. A perfect snack for all times.

1 pound (454 g) ground beef

½ pound (227 g) ground pork

½ pound (227 g) ground veal

1 cup freshly grated Romano cheese, plus more Romano for garnish

2 minced cloves garlic

2 eggs, whisked

Salt and ground black pepper, to taste

1½ tablespoons chopped Italian flat leaf parsley

2 cups shredded coconut

1½ cups lukewarm water

1 cup olive oil

1. In a large bowl, add the beef, pork, and veal. Stir to mix well. Add the cheese, whisked eggs, garlic, pepper, salt, and parsley. Blend well.
2. Add the coconut, then slowly add ½ cup water as you stir until the mixture is moist but still able to hold its

shape when rolled into meatballs. Form the mixture into 2-inch meatballs with your wet hands.

3. In a nonstick skillet, heat the olive oil, then fry the meatballs for about 15 minutes (in batches), turning occasionally, until evenly browned and slightly crispy.
4. Remove from the heat and sprinkle with Romano cheese on top for garnish, if desired.

STORAGE: Store in an airtight container in the fridge for up to 4 days or in the freezer for up to 1 month.

REHEAT: Microwave, covered, until the desired temperature is reached or reheat in a frying pan or air fryer / instant pot, covered, on medium.

SERVE IT WITH: To make this a complete meal, serve with Turmeric Beef Bone Broth.

PER SERVING

calories: 591 | fat: 49g | total carbs: 3.2g | fiber: 0.7g | protein: 33.1g

Stuffed Cheesy Mushrooms

Macros: Fat 76% | Protein 9% | Carbs 16%

Prep time: 25 minutes | Cook time: 20 minutes | Serves 3

A re you a mushroom lover? This is a delicious meal tailored just for you. The meal can turn to be your favorite as it is rich in flavors. It is a keto-friendly meal you will always enjoy.

12 whole fresh mushrooms

1 tablespoon olive oil

1 tablespoon minced garlic

1 (8-ounce / 227-g) package softened cream cheese

¼ teaspoon ground cayenne pepper

¼ teaspoon ground black pepper

¼ teaspoon onion powder

¼ cup grated Parmesan cheese

Cooking spray

1. Preheat the oven to 350ºF (180ºC) and spray a baking sheet with cooking spray. Set aside.
2. On a flat work surface, remove the mushroom stems, and finely chop them as you discard the tough stem endings. Reserve the mushroom caps on a plate.
3. In a nonstick skillet, heat the olive oil over medium heat. Add the chopped mushroom stems and garlic.

Fry them until all the moisture disappears, then transfer to a bowl to cool for 5 minutes.

4. Add the cream cheese, cayenne pepper, black pepper, onion powder and Parmesan cheese into the bowl of mushroom mixture. Stir thoroughly until well combined.
5. Using a spoon, stuff every mushroom cap with a considerable amount of the filling, then arrange the stuffed mushroom caps on the baking sheet.
6. Bake for about 20 minutes until the liquid starts to form under the caps and caps are piping hot.
7. Remove from the oven and serve warm on a plate.

STORAGE: Store in an airtight container in the fridge for up to 3 days.

REHEAT: Microwave, covered, until it reaches the desired temperature.

SERVE IT WITH: To make this a complete meal, serve with fresh salad greens or a side dish of your choice.

PER SERVING

calories: 361 | fat: 29.9g | total carbs: 16.6g | fiber: 2.0g | protein: 9.8g

Grilled Spicy Shrimp

Macros: Fat 75% | Protein 22% | Carbs 3%

Prep time: 30 minutes | Cook time: 10 minutes | Serves 6

This is a great recipe to enjoy. The oregano adds color and taste to the food. It takes a few minutes to cook. It is also spicy because of the hot pepper sauce.

1 cup plus 1 tablespoon olive oil

1 juiced lemon

¼ cup chopped fresh parsley

3 minced cloves garlic

2 tablespoons hot pepper sauce

2 teaspoons dried oregano

1 teaspoon ground black pepper

1 teaspoon salt

2 pounds (907 g) peeled and deveined large shrimp, tail-on

SPECIAL EQUIPMENT:

6 bamboo skewers (about 10 inches (25 cm) long), soaked for at least 30 minutes

1. Make the marinade: Combine 1 cup of olive oil, lemon juice, parsley, garlic, hot sauce, oregano, black pepper, and salt in a bowl. Stir well to incorporate.

2. Reserve some of the marinade for basting in a separate bowl. Pour the remaining marinade into a resealable plastic bag containing the shrimp. Shake and seal the bag, then transfer to the refrigerator and marinate for approximately 2 hours.
3. Preheat the grill to medium-low heat.
4. Thread the marinated shrimp onto the skewers, then discard the marinade.
5. Slightly oil the grill grates with 1 tablespoon of olive oil, then grill each side of the shrimp for about 5 minutes until the flesh is totally pink and opaque, basting frequently with the marinade you have reserved.
6. Cool for 5 minutes before serving.

STORAGE: Store in an airtight container in the fridge for up to 4 days or in the freezer for up to 1 month.

REHEAT: Microwave, covered, until it reaches the desired temperature.

SERVE IT WITH: To make this a complete meal, enjoy the grilled shrimp on a bed of greens.

PER SERVING

calories: 436 | fat: 37.6g | total carbs: 3.9g | fiber: 0.6g | protein: 21.0g

Red Pepper Roasted Dip

Macros: Fat 86% | Protein 11% | Carbs 3%

Prep time: 10 minutes | Cook time: 20 minutes | Serves 30

E njoy the amazing snack after a busy day. You can change the recipe by adding some walnuts to improve the taste and flavors. Try out this recipe and your cool evenings will never be the same.

1 tablespoon onion, minced

1 (7-ounce / 198-g) jar roasted red peppers , drained and diced

2 tablespoons Dijon mustard

1 (8-ounce / 227-g) package cream cheese, softened

¾ pound (340 g) shredded Monterey Jack cheese

1 garlic clove, minced

1 cup keto-friendly mayonnaise

1. Start by preheating the oven to 350 ºF (180 ºC)
2. Mix the onion, roasted red peppers, Dijon mustard, cream cheese, Monterey Jack cheese, garlic, and mayonnaise in a baking dish
3. Place in the prepared oven and bake for 20 minutes until lightly browned.
4. Remove from the oven and serve while still warm.

STORAGE: Store in an airtight container in the fridge for up to 1 week or in the freezer for up to 1 month.

REHEAT: Microwave, covered, until the desired temperature is reached or reheat in a frying pan or instant pot, covered, on medium.

SERVE IT WITH: To make this a complete meal, serve the dip with keto veggies.

PER SERVING

calories: 123 | fat: 12.2g | total carbs: 0.9g | fiber: 0.1g | protein: 3.1g

Buffalo Chicken and Cheese Dip

Macros: Fat 79% | Protein 17% | Carbs 4%

Prep time: 20 minutes | Cook time: 50 minutes | Serves 8

E njoy the tasty buffalo chicken and cheese dip snack at any time of the day. The meal is filled with rich cheese flavors that improve the texture and taste. You can prepare such snack and enjoy with family together or when friends visit.

2 bone-in chicken breast halves

1 teaspoon olive oil

1 stalk celery, finely diced

¾ cup ranch dressing

1 (8-ounce / 227-g) package softened cream cheese

¾ cup blue cheese dressing

⅓ cup hot pepper sauce

1 cup shredded Cheddar cheese

1. In a large saucepan, put the halved breasts and cover with water. Boil for 20 minutes until cooked through.
2. Remove the breasts from the pan. When cooled enough to handle, shred the meat and reserve them in a bowl.
3. Start by preheating the oven to 350 °F (180 °C)

4. In a large skillet, heat the olive oil until sizzling, then add the celery and fry until tender,
5. Add the ranch dressing, cream cheese, and blue cheese dressing.
6. Cook while stirring gently until creamy and smooth.
7. Add the shredded chicken and hot sauce. Stir to combine well.
8. Pour the mixture in a greased baking tray, then top with the shredded cheese.
9. Bake in the prepared oven until golden brown, for about 30 minutes.
10. Remove from the oven and serve hot.

STORAGE: Store in an airtight container in the fridge for up to 5 days or in the freezer for up to 1 month.

REHEAT: Microwave, covered, until it reaches the desired temperature. Do not overheat because it will look greasy.

SERVE IT WITH: To make this a complete meal, serve the buffalo chicken dip with celery sticks.

PER SERVING

calories: 430 | fat: 38.0g | total carbs: 3.9g | fiber: 0.2g | protein: 18.5g

Simple Broccoli Casserole

Macros: Fat 83% | Protein 6% | Carbs 11%

Prep time: 20 minutes | Cook time: 45 minutes | Serves 8

This is an easy-to-prepare recipe, filled with tasty flavors, creamy, and savory makes it stand out delicious. The touch of mushroom soup, cheese, and eggs makes the recipe perfect for dinner needs.

5 tablespoons butter, divided

1 chopped onion

2 (10-ounce / 284-g) packages chopped frozen broccoli, thawed

1 (11-ounce / 312-g) can condensed cream of mushroom soup

1 cup shredded sharp Cheddar cheese

1 cup mayonnaise, keto-friendly

2 beaten eggs

½ teaspoon garlic salt

¼ teaspoon ground black pepper

½ teaspoon seasoned salt

1½ teaspoons lemon juice

1. Start by preheating the oven at 350 °F (180 °C).
2. Put a medium saucepan over medium-high heat.

3. Melt 3 tablespoons of butter, then fry the onion to a gold brown color.
4. Mix the broccoli, eggs, lemon juice, onion, pepper, garlic salt, soup, seasoned salt, and cheese, mayonnaise in a mixing bowl. Top with the remaining 2 tablespoons of butter.
5. Place in the prepared oven and bake uncovered until the top starts to brown, for 45 minutes.
6. Remove from the oven and serve warm.

STORAGE: Store in an airtight container in the fridge for up to 3 days or in the freezer for up to three months.

REHEAT: Microwave, covered, until it reaches the desired temperature.

SERVE IT WITH: To make this a complete meal, serve the snack with pork tenderloins or chicken breast.

PER SERVING

calories: 606 | fat: 42.5g | total carbs: 42.5g | fiber: 21.9g | protein: 28.9g

Lightning Source UK Ltd.
Milton Keynes UK
UKHW020634220621
385949UK00001B/82

9 781803 176581